PASCAL'S FIRE

KRISTINA BRESNEN

Pascal's Fire

a poem

BIBLIOASIS
Windsor, Ontario

FIRST EDITION

Library and Archives Canada Cataloguing in Publication

Title: Pascal's fire / Kristina Bresnen.
Names: Bresnen, Kristina, author.
Description: Poems.
Identifiers: Canadiana (print) 20220465398 | Canadiana (ebook)
    2022046541X | ISBN 9781771965439 (softcover) | ISBN
    9781771965446 (EPUB)
Classification: LCC PS8603.R4685 P37 2023 | DDC C811/.6—dc23

Edited by Zachariah Wells
Copyedited by Emily Donaldson
Designed and typeset by Vanessa Stauffer
Cover image by Nastasic / IStockPhoto

Published with the generous assistance of the Canada Council for the
Arts, which last year invested $153 million to bring the arts to Canadians
throughout the country, and the financial support of the Government
of Canada. Biblioasis also acknowledges the support of the Ontario
Arts Council (OAC), an agency of the Government of Ontario, which
last year funded 1,709 individual artists and 1,078 organizations in
204 communities across Ontario, for a total of $52.1 million, and the
contribution of the Government of Ontario through the Ontario Book
Publishing Tax Credit and Ontario Creates.

PRINTED AND BOUND IN CANADA

For my family

SPEAKING IN TONGUES

Hestia lies in a hospital bed, lashes scabbed with sleep. Her feet push against the footboard and twist the sheets like kelp around her legs. I feed her water with a dropper and, when I look, I flinch to see her tongue, raw and caked with mucous. Scattered half-drunk cups of juice and tea, white carnations glowing buoyant in a bowl of water by the window. Her favourite shells lined up on a shelf, stones, keepsakes. Time passes in strange increments, plotless and thirsty. The light blurs, shimmer of heat above the clanking radiator. I see it bend, refract, displace itself.

This bed is a raft. At night it gets cold. I strap the planks with willow bark and punt off from the shore. I cover Hestia with a shawl and wait for morning throughout the watches of the night. I mark the time in red. I invent names for stars I do not know and watch them rise and set. I hold her hand for hours, and when I grow tired, I nod off against the bedrail.

§

To *hesitate*: from the Latin: to stick fast, stammer in
speech, be undecided.
To adhere, hold fast. Hold back in doubt or indecision.

§

Think of the tongue as a ship's rudder.

§

Once, I sat inside an abandoned hangar with two thousand people. A preacher exhorted us to speak in tongues, and so, together, two thousand voices clicked and groaned like small craft pitching in a storm. I sat, bewildered, and could not speak.

§

If anyone speak in a tongue, Paul tells the Corinthians, let one interpret.

§

From the Book of Exodus:

And Moses said unto the Lord, O Lord I am not eloquent, neither heretofore, nor since thou hast spoken unto thy servant: but I am of slow speech, and of a slow tongue. And the Lord said unto him, Who hath made man's mouth? or who maketh the dumb, or deaf, or the seeing, or the blind? Have not I the Lord? Now therefore go, and I will be thy mouth.

§

Sufi mystic, Shaykh al-'Alawī, recollecting the blind beggar crying out to Christ:

> The question of invocation is of wider scope than you imagine. A sick man lay groaning in the presence of the Prophet and one of the Companions told him to stop and to be patient, whereupon the Prophet said, "Let him groan, for groaning is one of the Names of God in which the sick man can find relief."

§

It is, say, the year 1253 B.C.E. Moses is herding his flock by the mountain of Horeb. All is well. He leads his sheep to the backside of the desert. No lions have torn them apart; each sheep is accounted for. Moses looks forward to seeing Zipporah. He looks forward to a meal of bean cake, cucumbers, leeks. But, a voice from a burning bush makes all desires drop. Each leaf, stippled with flame, seems to speak. Moses knows that along the usual edge of this kindled hour his life is now the careened hull of a ship going down.

Forget cucumbers. Forget leeks. The light turns silver and black. Moses grows cold, his mind dark as a cave. *Don't forget your crook*, Zipporah reminds him before going out. *Don't forget your cloak*.

What need of them here? Moses wonders.

§

Hestia once told me she preferred Moses to every other Biblical figure because he doubted, both his own words and the possibility of God's words. Maybe God chose Moses because he stuttered. His lips were shaped to God's, she said, or baffled by them, their words sparking off through the flame. Or maybe God chose Moses in this story because he turned aside to look. I don't know, she told me, but Moses refused almost everything God said to him.

Hestia holds doubt at a distance like a jewel, turning it this way and that, light bouncing off the facets. I watch the light across the hospital wall and follow its diffusions like a cat. "I will turn aside and see this great sight, why the bush is not burnt," says Moses, scoping out the wilderness.

§

Avivah Gottlieb Zornberg, a Torah scholar, on Moses:

> ...and whatever God says, he basically repudiates. It's the most extraordinary first meeting between God and a human being. It's not just that he's too modest to take on the role, he's skeptical about everything that God says. It's really almost what you would call *chutzpah*. It's just, how does one talk to God like that?

How indeed.

§

If my tongue were a ship's rudder, where would I go? How far? Where would my 'Yes' take me? Where my 'No'? Is it clarity I seek? Light? Vision? Certainty? Do I wish the low burn in my belly would cease so I could move freely, at ease? Or might I choose a safer course, talk about the weather where I am? Keep, like Hestia, the hearth fire lit? Prince Battus sought the Oracle at Delphi because of his stutter. The Oracle advised him to go abroad, build a city, and never come home. If I were a prince and told never to return to my kingdom, where would I go? How spend my days? To whom could I speak? Where might I find money to clothe and feed myself? How would I ask for directions? What particulars of rapture would call me to stay in or venture out?

§

According to a rabbinic legend, Moses, as a child, sat on Pharaoh's knee and stole his crown. Threatened, Pharaoh tested the child by placing a plate of onyx stone and burning coals in front of him. Moses reached for the stone, but the angel Gabriel, concealed, redirected the child's hand. And so, Moses lifted a lump of coal toward his tongue and burned it. It is understood that this was the cause of his stutter.

§

From the Book of Isaiah:

> Then flew one of the seraphim to me, having in his hand a burning coal which he had taken with tongs from the altar. And he touched my mouth…

§

Ali-Ibn-Abi-Talib, first cousin to Muhammad:

> A man is hid under his tongue.

§

Thomas Merton:

O my brother, the contemplative is not the one who
has fiery visions of the cherubim carrying God on their
imagined chariot, but simply he who has risked his
mind in the desert beyond language and beyond ideas
where God is encountered in the nakedness of pure
trust, that is to say in the surrender of our own poverty
and incompleteness in order no longer to clench our
minds in a cramp upon themselves, as if thinking made
us exist.

§

Moses opens the flap of his tent and goes up from the plains of Moab. There are sand sheets and seas, valleys and ridges, cliffs, ergs, and mountains. Barchan, seif, and star-shaped dunes ripple like waves. The sand is full of colour: quartz, diamond, olivine, bits of basalt from volcanoes. The surface is nudged and creeps. The wind picks up and lifts each grain; little shocks and volts bump against his skin and travel off. He brings with him his shoes, his staff, a vessel of water. Along steep paths he stumbles over burning rock, through saltbush, thistle. And beyond the Jordan valley he sees a land of palm trees, of figs and dates, of laurel and myrrh.

I think of Moses often. Think of that long stretch he turned with the Lord, like Abraham with his son, no going back. Palm fronds clack in the wind. Bits of rock stub themselves into burnt and blistered feet. I try and see what Moses saw: a land he'd have no business in. A land of giants, of milk and honey. Of reeds shaken by wind.

§

Zora Neale Hurston:

"No use talking," Jethro said to his wife. "Moses done found out something we others don't know about. Look like he done found the secret words that's the keys to God we all been looking for."

§

15

At Pentecost, so The Acts of the Apostles recounts, "there came a sound from heaven as of a rushing mighty wind, and it filled all the house where they were sitting. And there appeared unto them cloven tongues like as of fire, and it sat upon each of them."

Fire sparks from the muscled wind of a so-called heaven. Cloven tongues alight like sparrows on a branch, a blaze of wings furling all the leaves. Their twiggy feet click against the bark. A sound of licked fingers stubbing all the candles out, wick-singed skin. The heat catches at my throat. The house tilts like a ship inside the baffled current of a storm, the prow tipped and breaking. There is the tilting, but so too the aftermath, the slip of moon behind the cloud, a quiet wrack of mist. The still and certain dark.

§

Rilke:

Flare up like flame
    and make big shadows I can move in

§

A.R. Ammons:

If I find you I will have to leave the earth
and go on out

§

The hangar is clammy, packed, charged. It sings and howls. Hands are raised and clap and reach out to some person I can't see. Arms shake and twitch. Bodies fall backward. From this vaulted place, I hear a tremulous sound: the lone voice of a woman, crying. Her cries climb into the steel trusses, the brace rods, the ridge vents, a gauzed strand of smoke wreathing up around the beams. A sound unlike any I have heard. It strains against the other sounds like creaking trees against the wind. My body all weather, rumbling through the floor so many rows apart. I lean in. Tender and nerved, hum and groan, I feel for something that may never come to speech.

I know only this: I am out here on the fringes. I bank my wings into the turn and lift.

§

Saint Jerome, in a letter to Heliodorus:

The desert loves to strip bare.

§

I want to hear Hestia speak, the *glóssa* of the land where
she lives now, almost gone from me: a single word, any,
unremarkable; not the fringe of time inside that hangar,
that pressure of sound and wind like a tree whipped back,
not that; not consolation, or assurance, or her thoughts
that read my own like glass; not proof of worlds she sees
or doesn't see beyond the desert of this room, sounds she
does or doesn't hear, I don't need that; or maybe that,
some piece, a hint, a rudiment of prayer to teach me
how to hear, translate, elucidate, but all the prayers I say
inside this room I don't believe, so no, but something *like*
that, or just the darkened silence of this room, the closest
thing we share, but all I hear is the *drip-drip* of the I.V.
pump and her feet pushing up against the bedrail and,
anyway, who am I to tell her what to speak?

§

Ammons:

And I know if I find you I will have to stay with the
earth.

§

The Hebrew word *midbar*: in the sense of driving; a
pasture (i.e., open field, where cattle are driven); by
implication, a desert; also speech (including its organs):—
desert, speech, wilderness.

§

November 23rd, 1654: Blaise Pascal sits in a rented flat on the rue des Francs-Bourgeois. He has his deck of cards, his dice, a lantern gear, his metal wheels. Stars craze and burn across the pitch. He flanks the rock ledge of his bivouac. He writes the word FIRE in bold and sews the word inside his coat where, after his death, a servant will discover it. How long does he keep watch, pacing within the four walls of his flat, before that kindled hour strikes at half past ten? At half past ten, what reverie announces itself, what joy, dread? He forgets his learning. Forgets all of Euclid's propositions. Conic sections. Binomial expansions, their rows and rows. The light turns silver and black. What fire burns there in the dark, the rock ledge of his room, leaf-littered?

§

I'll never know. I'll never see what Pascal saw. I see Hestia
in her hospital bed. I see blisters on her back the size of
hockey pucks. I see black bile I mistake for blood and
wipe it with a kleenex. "Oh, that's just what's left of her
stomach, love," the nurse tells me when I ask. I forget all
my learning. Forget grammar, syntax. I feel a burning
in my throat and hear the dry-erase brush *swish* against
the whiteboard. It is half past ten in the evening, smell of
disinfectant in the air. I pace the boards of my raft and
drift unmoored without pole or rudder. I try and see what
Hestia sees, but can't. I watch her turn and turn and bind
her blazing wounds with gauze.

I make rough stitchery of conversion.

§

John Berryman:

Who can search Thee out?

except Isaiah & Pascal, who saw.
I dare not ask that vision ...

I dare not ask it either.

§

It began with a simple question: What is it that you want?
And the blind man replied, I want to see.

And behold, he saw.

§

Hans Urs von Balthasar:

> The better a man learns to pray, the more deeply he
> learns that all his stammering is only an answer to
> God's speaking to him.

I want to know what this means.

§

Marilyn Monroe was advised to speak in a breathy voice to help keep her stutter in check. She wrote:

> To this day I stutter once in a while. Hardly anyone notices. It only happens when I get excited and nervous inside. I try my darnedest not to, but sometimes I do.

§

On average, a person speaks between one hundred and twenty and one hundred and eighty words per minute.

§

Martin Buber:

> It is laid upon the stammering to bring the voice of Heaven to earth.

§

Augustine:

> And I babbled unto Thee my brightness, my riches, my health ...

§

At Hestia's bedside I call God by different names.
Sometimes God is Wind and sometimes God is Fire Shut
Up in My Bones. Sometimes Holy Heart Wrencher,
Inmost Eyes Unseen. Sometimes Inmost, Utmost,
Passing Stranger, Breathless Bounding In, Bringer Inner
of Sprite, Secret Place of Thunder. Sometimes I curl up
in the dark by Hestia's side, her breath like God's own,
and call Him Hush, Sigh. Reverie. Fright. He Who Hides
in the Dark. Sometimes, I don't know. Sometimes God
flies in like a cardinal as if we were His home. Sometimes
He goes out. Sometimes I ask Him to go.

§

Gregory of Nyssa:

> When we give a thing a name we imagine we have got a
> hold of it. We imagine that we have got a hold of being.
> Perhaps we should do better not to flatter ourselves too
> soon that we can name God.

§

While tending Hestia, listening for her voice that isn't there, listening for God's, I read Flaubert's "A Simple Heart." Félicité, that unlettered housemaid some would call stupid, her parrot by her side, her heart like a blue, blue sky, and her mind—well, "to a mind like hers," writes Flaubert, "the supernatural appears perfectly ordinary." It's unclear whether this voice condescends to minds "like hers" or applauds, because, of course, right then, Félicité's mind is fixed, for two whole nights, on Virginie's dead body, and she wonders—kissing her—if Virginie's eyes will open. She believes they could, "she would not have been in the least surprised" if they did, but, of course, they don't, and never will again.

§

Sayings of the Desert Fathers:

Abbot Bessarion, dying, said, "the monk should be all eye, like the cherubim and seraphim."

§

It was cold. A canticle rose, dropped to a chant, and
the nave stilled. A woman began to speak in a tongue I
couldn't understand. The pews creaked. Light poured
through the windows, throwing shadows of leaves on the
floor. Radiators clanked and hissed. I didn't believe it,
but did: something took over. A voice not her own, but
her own, mounting, teasing vowels from root, headwater,
twig. The liquids and mutes, like cuts of ice swept
downstream. What was she saying? What pitch was she
tuned to? She halted and the room went aphonic, save
for a hum like a powerline snapped. After the halt, after
the hum like a current, after the air turned quiet again
and the radiators stopped clanking; days later, or years, a
confusion occurred in my head and abides there: Moses
just whispered his own stuttered song in her ear.

§

Anna Kamienska:

I'm open to all annunciations.

§

In one dream—aslant on the splintered timber of my raft, head against the bedrail—Félicité digs through a wide arc of land strewn with red dust, bones, and shells. As in Georgia O'Keeffe's paintings, some bones are outsized, dwarfing the hills. The hills are painted ochre, glacier-blue and purply-red, like the blisters on Hestia's back; their slopes resemble folds of skin. Félicité walks up and down the slopes, her body all eye, feet treading the blue, blue grass, the desert marigold. Dust, dust, dust. She brings back fossils: brachiopods, corals. She brings bones: skulls, pelvis, rib. They feel endless, those bones. She spreads them across the grass, sun-bleached and tinted rust. She holds one up like a viewfinder and peers through its hole to a sky that looks back, empty, pacific. "That blue that will always be there," O'Keeffe says in my dream, a voice out of nowhere, speaking like God. And in my dream, the bones hear her too, those bones that hope for nothing.

§

"The whole creation groans," writes Paul.

What is this utterance?

§

Hestia tells me the thoughts of her heart. Full of pauses,
her words quiver like tulle floating in a lake. Her upper lip
twitches.

It might be I am Nobody, she says.
It could be I am lost as Moses in the desert.
Strange, how the thought of him—
who saw the shape of God's back, the dark of it
a slip of moon across the sun—
should bring consolation.
He of cloud and fire.
He of the tongue-tied.
The dumbstruck.
Why do the marks of his weakness
comfort me? Some nights I weep,
afraid, she tells me.
The wind bristles my hair and skin
and there is nothing to cover myself with,
after all. I hear God's footsteps fall lightly
over the damp earth. "Where are you?" He asks,
tone yielding and soft.
Why did you make me scared? I ask God.
These thoughts. These words like little sails.
Thistle. A hawk moth's hover.
O Moses, she says,

and falls asleep against her pillow.

§

Emily Dickinson:

In all the Circumference of Expression, those guileless
words of Adam and Eve were never surpassed, "I was
afraid and hid myself."

§

If the vocal cords, back of the tongue and velum, middle
of the tongue and hard palate, tongue tip and upper front
teeth, upper front teeth and lower lip, or upper and lower
lips were to partially block the breath stream, the rhythm
and rate of speech would be altered.

§

Dr. Dieffenbach thought that the source of the stutter was the tongue itself, and so he cut "triangular wedges" from the mouths of many patients. He envisioned a world in which precise instruments would be developed to facilitate such operations and imagined his life filled with metal tools, "knives and scissors with improved curves, and a thousand variously fashioned forceps and hooks." As Benson Bobrick recounts, all operations were conducted without anesthesia. With one successful patient, a boy of thirteen, Dr. Dieffenbach writes that he "was exceedingly pleased to hear him pronounce words which, previous to the operation, he was unable to articulate." According to Bobrick the boy said, fluently, "there is some blood running down my shirt."

§

Irish Jesuit William Doyle, an army chaplain who died in the Battle of Ypres, practiced the art of prayer known as Aspirations. In 1909, calling upon the name of Christ, Doyle murmured several thousand Aspirations a day. By 1916, he felt called to an abundance: "Again a clear interior light that God wants me to aim at 100,000 Aspirations daily. I feel a longing to take up this life of unceasing prayer and at the same time a dread and loathing of this burden."

§

Dr. Dieffenbach sets out across the desert. He carries his bag of tools: his hooks, his forceps, his scissors. He has brought water, and a blanket. The bag of tools he hugs tight while he sleeps. During the day his instruments clang against each other, a metallic music. There is nothing here. When the sun is at its zenith he pitches the blanket like a tent and hides beneath it. His tongue is parched and caked with mucous. He falls asleep with sand in his eyes and in the morning wakes to someone nudging him, a plate of food near his head. He rubs the sand and sleep from his eyes but sees nothing. He eats and eats.

It has been years.

§

Around the time of the 1906 earthquake what some called a "latter rain" fell on the Azusa Street revival. Passersby witnessed a glow emanating from the church: an ocean's luminescence in the night, plankton like stars assembling on the shore. One member described the room like people "slain in battle." "A forest of fallen trees," another said. Their voices were heard throughout the stockyards, the stables, the tenements, and tombstone shops. The latter rain of speech is what some called it, for it felt like freshness, the language of dew and grass. Tongues and lips "moved and twisted about" with the riot of their praise in the latter rain of those days before the house collapsed.

§

I set out across the desert to remove the cramp upon my mind. I unearth bone tools, burins, awls. I put out into the deep, tie the head-ropes, cast the nets. Here, the ancient waters that lie beneath the sands: the lakes, the stream floodplains, the marshes and grasslands. There, the ancient vessels that travelled along: shrub boats and lashed planks, leaf-netted carriers. I lose myself in caves, my hair dreadlocked and stinking, my feet smoothed to glass with the sand's burnishing and the sun's long heat. I bring my metal tools: my hooks, forceps, scissors. I bring my musical repertoire, my blanket.

§

Simone Weil:

We have to be in a desert. For he whom we must love is absent ... We must be rooted in the absence of place.

§

Song of Songs:

I sought him whom my soul loves; I sought him, but found him not.

§

Heart-sore, I wait. I see a night full of fog. I hear a sound like the buried bells of churches pealing out from the dunes. I abide the again-making of my body. And the earth abides—barchan, seif, star—and the wind carves infinitesimal craters into everything. I gaze off into trackless air, gritty with sand. Locusts jumping in the dark. What is this groaning? I know if I find you—here, now—I won't have found you. Not here, not now. And so, I wait. I pitch my blanket like a tent and hide beneath it. I speak, on average, between one hundred and twenty and one hundred and eighty words per minute, but there emanates from my mouth something I can't articulate. A thing loosed, travailing.

§

Virginia Woolf, "Bernard" *The Waves*

> I need a little language such as lovers use, words of one syllable such as children speak when they come into the room and find their mother sewing and pick up some scrap of bright wool, a feather, or a shred of chintz. I need a howl; a cry.

§

I was once instructed in the gift of tongues. To begin,
move your tongue as though gargling salt water. You'll
feel stupid, I was told. No matter. The spirit will soon
intercede. I tried it. Alone in my room I bent my head
and shut my eyes and uttered low murmurings. I moved
my tongue as though gargling salt water.

I felt stupid.

§

John 3:8:

The wind bloweth where it listeth.

§

The wind has picked up. Eddies of sand stretch to meet
the clouds, swarming like locusts. I wrap my scarf around
my face and squint and squint and run for cover under
a quiver tree. Next to me, a woman with a red skirt and a
kerchief pinned to her hair shouts above the storm's roar,
"I'm Nobody, who are you?" Félicité. Objects fly past
her: snake husks, mollusk shells, the bones of a gazelle.
A shell nicks her chin. She yells and dances and sings and
gestures me to join her. As she sings "One Silver Dollar"
I *tap tap tap* my wooden timbrel in time.

§

I want to say what I mean, dig out the one word. Water
drips from stalactites. Cold air rushes along the corridors,
my skin feels peeled back. Where my headlamp shines, I
see figures painted in red. Calcite glistens like candle wax.
Columns fill each gallery—giant organs and dinosaur
bones, heaps of gypsum like shark teeth. An old wolf
howl is trapped in the air, and I try to catch it, that song,
with my trowel and brush, my pickaxe and spade. It is a
groaning sound. Of wind. Of breath hovering over black
waters.

§

I am here by a cave and the jackdaws are crowing.
Jackrabbits graze and gopher snakes wait in sandy washes.
Grasshopper shells, pinched and chewed, pile up at my
feet. Hunched on the ground, I murmur and groan when
I hear a light clatter of stones. Out of the cave appears a
man. He grinds tree root to make porridge and, kneeling,
hands it to me in a small wooden bowl. He lays his hand
on my shoulder. What is it that you want? he asks. His
breath smells of figs and hickory root, his skin is the colour
of wood shavings, singed at the edges. I tell him I want
to speak with the tongue of men and angels. I tell him I
want my words to sound like jewels being raked over with
bright, regal hands. I eat and eat and lay the bowl down.
When I look up the man is gone.

§

> Likewise the Spirit also helps in our weakness. For
> we do not know what we should pray for as we ought,
> but the Spirit Himself makes intercession for us with
> groanings which cannot be uttered.

These are the words of Paul. I don't really understand
this passage but there is humility in it, and gentleness, this
acknowledgment that something other than our words
can hold us, that our groaning is significant. My mind's
not always right. Try as I might, I can't comprehend or
reckon with each ache or thought or qualm, every word
laid from end to end like clothes blown out on a line. And
oh, these words I think I know and dress in, arrange and
rearrange. *Oh*, I cry as the clouds heave in. *Oh*.

§

Psalm 81:10:

> Open thy mouth wide and I will fill it.

§

Moses:

Please, O Lord, I am not a man of words.

§

And yet, and yet, God and Moses speak "mouth-to-mouth" the Book of Numbers declares. No riddles, not in dark speech. They speak as two people living in the same house. God lets Moses walk through the door of His own inviolable Self, a gust down the mountain like a welt of cold across the waste, and there they sit, or stand, or kiss (as I once construed that phrase), or brace themselves inside the woe and weal of God's stark weather, now blinding, now light as air stirring a wind vane. Through that intimate veil, an intake of breath. Hidden in the nook of a cave or the hush of a cloud, who knows what Moses speaks and hears?—what halts and exaltations, turning of words like clove on the tongue, snow, sleet, honey, rue, the pang of a word that won't come, the coming up for air. But the Israelites can't accompany him—can't hear those sounds, endure that light and pressure. Other than Moses, who could? In all his hesitations, the repeated negations, disarticulations—*if, but, not, won't*—it is Moses' mouth, not another's, as Zornberg points out, that God wants. Tongue as precipice. Tongue as site of longing. God hears "the groaning of the Israelites," He says to Moses. And the groaning goes to God—that Form that can't and won't be touched, shapeshifting, ineffable—and more than hearing, more than echo from some wildered, measureless distance, there is, it feels, an unseen body open, pressing through, mouth-to-mouth.

§

Dr. Dieffenbach rushes along in his great white coat, his skin burnt from the sun. As he passes by, I tell him he ought to be wearing a hat, and would he like mine? He scrunches up his face. Maybe embarrassed. Maybe he once had the ill-fortune of having to put up with someone who could not utter articulate voice and consequently set out to cure this uncomfortable condition. And so he goes headlong into the world with his little tools, his hooks and forceps, scalpels and scissors, and his life is measured by the precision of his incisions, the number of triangular wedges he carries in his bag. And along comes Moses now. Dr. Dieffenbach and Moses meet and the doctor suggests that Moses would be an excellent candidate for this procedure he has been developing. Moses thinks for a moment and hesitates and shifts on his feet and his staff keeps turning into a snake, even when he does not mean for it to, and his hair is white and his face is dazzling and his robes are long and billowing and finally, *finally*, thinks Dr. Dieffenbach, Moses says... *no*. Dr. Dieffenbach is stunned that such a man could ever have been a prophet, because he stutters so, and does not know how to handle his staff.

§

Paul, in his letter to the Corinthians, describes a "thorn" in his flesh. He asks Christ three times to remove it. No one knows the precise nature of this thorn. Paul never names it. Theories abound: violent headaches, leprosy, a speech impediment, epilepsy, ophthalmia. Still others suggest struggles of a different kind. The particulars do not matter. Whatever the nature of this thorn, he cannot abide it and seeks to rid his body of it. Christ does not remove it.

§

Emily Dickinson:

Not to discover weakness is
the Artifice of strength—

§

I discover a shipwreck. Long burnt from the sun, its steel hull is rusted and the gun turret mounted. The barrels point west across the sand and seem alive enough. In the evening scorpions scuttle where I sleep, their pincers swollen and keeled. I spend three days and three nights inside this rusted hulk. On the third night I hear a humming sound, aft of the bridge. It is a dying woman. Her face is pale and gaunt and jewelled rings adorn each hand. She hums and gestures me to join her in her song, though I do not know the words, for it is Greek, and she is Hestia. Her tongue is raw and caked with mucous. I sit with her until the sun rises in the east and feed her water with a dropper. She thanks me by blowing kisses and I wipe her forehead with my hands. When she dies, I rest with her body three days.

On the third, the animals close in.

§

Edward Abbey:

Whether we live or die is of absolutely no concern whatsoever to the desert.

§

Psalm 44:19:

You have broken us in the place of jackals.

§

Paul steps onto the isthmus, sand clinging to his feet.
His eyes burn with salt water and as he walks, he groans.
He holds nothing in his hands and has no bag. His shoes
long lost, his body flecked with scabs. Plinths line the
Lechaion Road. Hermes sits there, Artemis, Poseidon.
The Fountain of Pereine. The howls of dogs echo off the
columns through the stoas; votives light the casements
here and there. A smell of kelp, meat, celeriac. In fear
and trembling, Paul brings his violent headaches, his
leprosy, his red, swollen eye, his words budging the tip
of his salted tongue. He resolves to know nothing save his
Lord's agony.

§

On the beach, the man with breath like figs and hickory
root gathers jetsam from the wreck into a basket: a
shoe, crates of ruined fruit, plastic bottles, a small plush
bird. A charcoal fire burns behind him. Smell of fish,
cakes of bread. Trembling, I drop my gear—my pickaxe,
spade, blanket—turn towards the fire and slump across
the sand, belly cool against the shore. I lie like this for
hours, bloodshot, restless, blank. I hear the waves rise and
ebb along their way, shifting sand. Seaweed drifts in the
current, anemones, seashells, crabs; old bones of buried
harbours, ropes, anchors; the washed-up bricks of sunken
cities. When I look back, the man is gone, a plate of food
near my head.

§

When God asks Moses to free his people, Moses pleads to be released from the task because, he says, he speaks with "faltering lips." It is too heavy, too much, this thing that God asks. And he believes God has made a mistake. He begs that Aaron, his brother, be his mouthpiece. So Aaron becomes his stand-in, the means by which Moses navigates the space between the world within and the world without.

§

Moses opens the flap of his tent and goes up from the plains of Moab to the place where the Lord will bury him. He brings his shoes, his staff, a vessel of water. Along steep paths he stumbles over burning rock, through saltbush, thistle. Beyond the valley he sees a land of palm trees, of laurel and myrrh, of giants and honey. He smashes beetles with his fist against the stones and chews and spits their green and armoured backs. He considers the land as a tongue feels for water in a scorched, loved place, and the wind scatters the rushes, and the saltbush bristles.

§

Emily Dickinson:

> It always felt to me—a wrong
> To that Old Moses—done—
> To let him see—the Canaan—
> Without the entering—

Me too.

§

I would like to have here with me a mouthpiece through whom my words and prayers might be interpreted because I do not know what to speak or what to pray for or how or why, though there exists inside me a groaning I can't articulate. What is this groaning? I am waiting.

§

Psalm 5:1:

> Give ear to my words, O Lord; give heed to my groaning.

§

Aslant on the splintered timber of my raft, my feet
propped against the bedrail, I wake. Flaubert's *Three Tales*
lies flat against my chest. My mind like a sieve, I forget
what tale I am reading. Julian? Herodias? I forget where
I am. The stripped bed lies empty. It is dark, halogen
light cants in through the cracks, the blue light of dusk
through the window. Dusk, dusk, dusk. What day is it?
What year? Where is Hestia? I look behind the curtain,
in the bathroom. The man with skin the colour of wood
shavings walks through the door. He holds a styrofoam
cup full of water, a small plush bird. I ask him where
Hestia is. I don't know, I don't know, though I can't
tell whose voice is speaking. I ask him his name, but he
doesn't say. Why won't he say his name? My voice grates
against the air, the air so blue and dark, the dark so full
of sounds, *drip-drip*, *beep-beep-beep*, shuffle of feet in the
hall. I hate those sounds, the stupid, terrible light. Who
are you? I ask the man, over and over, punching the bed
with my fist, the pillows, the sheets stripped—gone, gone,
gone. What day is it? Is it night? The man with breath
like figs offers me water, but I'm not thirsty, and how can
I drink? Rain slants against the window and the flowers
offend on their sills—carnations, hydrangeas—buoyant
and bright. Ditto the bird, ditto the shells lined up on the
shelf, stones, cold fossils intoning faint traces of life—but
things have to die first. I drink and drink and fall asleep
against the pillow. He covers my arms with a shawl and
waits with me for morning throughout the watches of the
night. He marks the time in red.

§

So be it, then. So be it.
The wind sighs through the mustard tree,
the olive, the cedar,
making little furrows of the streams.
Stray light, grasses bent in the dusk.
          O Hestia, I cry. O heart of my own heart,
home.
Whatever doubt or grief, whatever travail,
heart-sore and loosed,
I quicken. I glory in the falter.
Whatever tools I bring to cloak
or obviate the frightened nerve, the low
burning in my belly,
I cede them.
I punt off from the shore, the marshes, the grasslands.
The inlets widen before me, my raft a splintered vessel,
no matter.
My hunger lays me bare and in the dark
          a sparrow brings me food,
feathers brushing the lashed planks, and though I cannot see it,
          I rest in its sufficiency; here,
now. The night invisible:
clouds, waters, seaweed drifting in the current.
          And in the drift
a glow arises from the deep: the blue-green light
of fish, blooming algae, ormers, sea urchins,
charged particles of waves,
neon in the pitch.

§

Not far from shore, Moses and Félicité drink from a
stream, weeds drifting in the current like hair. They drink
and drink. When they are done, she shows Moses her
treasures and kitsch: her cheap religious prints, her book
of geography, artificial flowers, shells, her parrot's blue
feather—the colour of sky, lapis lazuli. Moses brushes
the feather through his outstretched hand and holds it
up to the sun. "That's from the Holy Ghost," she tells
him. "Ah, yes, of course," he says, and asks to see more;
her plush hat, her ribbons. He shows her his hands, now
leprous and white, now living. He shows her the words of
his tongue, hieroglyphs, flame. I hear them laughing—at
what, I don't know. They whisper to each other, her hand
cupped to his ear, his ear bent to her mouth. Orange trees
everywhere, fig, date, green garlands, bridge lines of
cobwebs like lace. Foxgloves, hydrangeas. She kisses his
eyes and his cheek and they fall asleep in the sand, those
dunes so full of colour: quartz, diamond, olivine, bits
of basalt from volcanoes. Little shocks and volts bump
against their skin and travel off.

§

Song of Songs:

Let him kiss me with the kisses of his mouth.

§

Heart-sore, I wait, wander, muck about, glean the beach
for stones. No burning coal has ever touched my mouth
and, no, "I dare not ask that vision, though a piece of
it," yes, a piece is—in harsher climes—bestowed. I wear
it. Hold it near as a keepsake, a coat. Or near as a word
on my tongue. Or near as a flame, but not so near as
that—nearer the heat it gives out. Sometimes I place it,
light as a bird's egg, in the dent of a crag and watch the
wind shake it. When I wake in the morning, it's there.
The hours go by, the years—my eyes and teeth gritty with
sand—and the sun burns my skin, the granite and schist.
Some hours incise. Some temper with cloud or the shade
of a tree, the leaves of acacia. In the cool, you turn at the
edge of my sight like a fox skirting the shrub, tracking the
breeze. Some hours are mischief, lark. The ravens fly off
at the sound of my laughing. *Come back!* I yell at the blue,
the birds, the play of dusk on their feathers. Some hours,
I'm nudged into sleep. At night, the dunes make a sound
like the chords of a cello, or foghorns, or bells, or a
plane clipping the ridge of a hill with its wing. Sometimes,
nothing. A landslip. Static. Either way, the sounds move
about like voices off the rib vault of a roof, and I bend my
ear to the timbre. Quiet, close.

§

The Lord is burying Moses somewhere near Moab,
no one knows where. Before Moses died, they climbed
Mount Nebo together, crossed the plains of Moab to
the top of Pisgah, across from Jericho. The Lord showed
Moses the whole land, the land sworn to his forefathers.
From Gilead to Dan, all of Naphtali, Judah, as far as the
Western Sea. There are terebinth groves, where Moses is
being buried, and the faint scent of mint carried through
long grass where grasshoppers live. The Lord pours oil
over stones and places the stones at Moses' head. He
hands small stones to Dr. Dieffenbach, whose coat is
covered in blood, and to Félicité, whose chin is flecked
with scabs.

§

Dr. Dieffenbach places his hand in the pocket of his great white coat and there is a clanking of metal instruments. It startles him. He seems to have forgotten they were there. He walks over to where the Lord stands. As Dr. Dieffenbach bends down to place a stone at Moses' head, a scalpel falls from his pocket into the dirt, and there is a scattering of mustard seed. This is no place to come when there is blood on your shirt, thinks Dr. Dieffenbach to himself, but here he is, with Félicité, and with the Lord, whose hands are full of stones. No one knows where Moses is being buried, no one knows what world, but it is hard by a cave, and the jackdaws are crowing.

§

Paul is here, with his red, swollen eye. His hair smells
of kelp, shoes lost to shipwreck ages ago. Thank you, he
says to the Lord, whose hands are full of oil; He kisses
Paul's forehead, his mouth, and his eyes. Félicité holds
a box made of shells, foxgloves, one blue feather. Hestia
wipes the sleep from her lashes and covers my arms with
a shawl. I write the word FIRE in bold and give the word
to the Lord. He places it in a small wooden bowl. It keeps
us warm throughout the watches of the night. We each
remove our shoes, and the wind blows through the leaves,
and the saltbush bristles. Grasshoppers twitch in the grass.

§

I sit, bewildered, inside an abandoned hangar. Together,
two thousand tongues clatter and groan like creaking
trees against the wind, a blaze of wings furling all the
leaves. Small fires kindled here. The light I sew inside my
coat.

§

Think of the tongue as a ship's rudder.

§

To *hesitate*: from the Latin: to stick fast, stammer in speech, be undecided.

§

To hold back in doubt:

§

The word I most often falter over is my own name.

NOTES

11 *God chose Moses ... because he turned aside to look.* This
is a Midrashic observation glossed by Avivah Gottlieb
Zornberg in her commentary *The Particulars of
Rapture: Reflections on Exodus.*

12 *Prince Battus sought the Oracle at Delphi ...* My sketch
of Battus is a corrupt version of Herodotus' account.

20 *The Hebrew word midbar ...* This is a direct citation
from Strong's Hebrew Lexicon of the Bible.

26 *While tending Hestia ... I read Flaubert ...* I am indebted
to philosopher James K. A. Smith, whose reading of
Flaubert's "A Simple Heart" in his book *Thinking in
Tongues* informed and enlivened my own. The poem's
question regarding the narrator's equivocal stance
toward Félicité is raised similarly by Smith.

32 *Irish Jesuit William Doyle ...* Doyle is quoted in *Prayer:
A History*, by Philip Zaleski and Carol Zaleski. I draw
on their biographical details.

36 *... the buried bells of churches ...* I borrow this phrase
from Michael Welland's *Sand: The Never-Ending Story.*

ACKNOWLEDGMENTS

Thank you to The Canada Council for the Arts and the Conseil des Arts et des Lettres du Québec for their generous support during the writing of this book. I am grateful to the Sage Hill Poetry Colloquium for a glorious ten days. My heartfelt thanks to Ken Babstock, Heidi Greco, Katherine Lawrence, Joanna Lilley, and Mitch Spray. In altered form, *Speaking in Tongues* was short-listed for a CBC Literary Awards competition in 2007. I am thankful for this encouragement in the early development of the poem.

To the friends and readers who offered their time and insight over the years, David Hickey, David K. O'Hara, Anne Simpson, Holly Lomheim, Fay Strohschein, and Martine Wizman, my profound gratitude. Special thanks to Ross Leckie, who first encouraged me to keep writing this poem before I knew what it was; to Jeremiah Webster, who guided an earlier version of this manuscript with wisdom and kindness, and Kristin Webster for the long walks and rich conversation.

Thanks to Dan Wells, Vanessa Stauffer, Emily Donaldson, and everyone at Biblioasis. And thank you to my editor, Zachariah Wells, for his intelligence, careful attention, and commitment.

A big thank you to my parents, Ken and Ruth, and my brother, Jeremy, and his family: you are my joy. And finally, Johan, my liefie, dankie vir jou onwrikbare geloof in my en al die lag.

KRISTINA BRESNEN is from Montreal and currently lives in Vancouver. *Pascal's Fire* is her first book.